Steam-Cleaning Love

 J.A. HAMILTON

Brick Books

CANADIAN CATALOGUING IN PUBLICATION DATA

Hamilton, J.A. 1954-
  Steam-cleaning love

Poems.
ISBN 0-919626-68-8

I. Title.

PS8565.A556S74 1993   C811'.54   C93-095041-0
PR9199.3.H35S74 1993

Acknowledgements: I would like to thank the Ontario Arts
Council for generous assistance, as well as the following journals
for first publishing some of these poems: *Malahat Review* and
American Voice. 'the body's memory' and 'Silver Pennies' are from
Body Rain (Brick Books, 1991). 'Steam-Cleaning Love' was
published in *Vintage 92* (League of Canadian Poets, 1992).
'Seaweed' appeared in *Snapshots: The New Canadian Fiction* (Black
Moss Press, 1992).

I am deeply indebted to Stan, Marnie, Kitty, John and Sue.

The support of the Canada Council and the Ontario Arts Council
is gratefully acknowledged. The support of the Government of
Ontario through the Ministry of Culture, Tourism and Recreation
is also gratefully acknowledged.

Cover design and artwork by Sheila Norgate.

Typeset in Ehrhardt, printed and bound by The Porcupine's
Quill. The stock is acid-free Zephyr Antique laid.

Brick Books
Box 38, Station B
London, Ontario
N6A 4V3

The pressure is women
holding my hand

This book is for them

Contents

How We Are Counted

That Old Means-Everything

Window Box of Bruises

Blue
for Corbin

When you came to town
you were in an envelope
I opened you
in the way of women opening women
I let you loose at False Creek
riding the seesaw
The day was full of blue
blue water
and blue ducks waddling the lawn

I was very happy
I turned on the sun
undid it gently
and wrapped you inside
blue fire

I was looking for words
I ran to the beach
I climbed the lifeguard tower
and pumped-up there
throwing blue to gulls
All the boats in the harbour
capsized
The mountains jigged
enormous shoulders –
what a scene

I sting with kisses I don't send
Not love, then –
the past is elastic and snaps

I was 35
It was the middle, a corner
This birthday cake is
wrapped in blue wax
I send it along
to an American address

Words are an apportionment
Wild, you say and maybe it stops
I would gladly be frightened
instead of tired

On Sunday the fire
sat under stockings
looking at the snow
It was your birthday
It was December and blue
I couldn't squeeze the distance
to tell you so myself

the body's memory
for dk

    fertility oils. someone is a bear in the corner sucking in a
fist.
    all the cunts in the world and every piano key depressed.
    apple pulp in september the music says.
    the music says tissue is an edible pink.
    rat a tat tat ribald and racy *oh la.* some woman's uterus a
bitten plum. someone is a red
    jet setter.
    colour develops babies. cellos burp. every infant
    is a rite a rite
    a streak of paint linen oil on canvas
    baby i
    i
    am a tongue.

    fourteen fierce nights, a succulent pear, a hand larger than
a head. scars.
    a woman sitting on a hill holding an orgasm holding a wrist.
    a piano on a hill. on top a woman spreads her legs and
splits into cunt and bear.

    the moon spits a hundred sorrows into sunrise. bleeds
fingers of yellows and blues. bends spoons.
    women roll their lovers over jackpots.

    i open my stomach to her. she paints with my blood clots and
bone.
    the flute is my throat wobbling. someone a bear –

Apology
for S

1 Eventually I was the liar,
the one who turned over,
who offered the kiss,
the rapture.

I who should have known,
who walked through valleys
of fools
lighting candles.

I who balanced memory
on a tightrope of desire,
I who flew in beautiful tights,
radiant as sunrise.

2 I betrayed you easily
as rain falls, as earth thirsts,
my fledgling hunger
parting its beak

for the worm, for the kiss,
the satisfying thrust.
You were less than a shadow:
I mocked you.

At night I bedded
scorn and righteousness,
lapping victory between their legs,
my tongue long.

Forecast
for Brook

This is the entranceway, the foyer,
the place to leave your shoes.
The floor tiles buckle.
Horizontal, I am ready.
I am unnaturally stirred,
an eye on the tiles, staring up at you,
blinking wildly.

Intimacy is a matter of shutters
clacking in hurricane wind, open and shut
like books, open and shut, like mouths,
open and shut, like hearts pumping
to a rhythm devised in utero.
There is a time to hold a tongue perfectly still,
and I have found it, it is instinctual,
it can crack a rose-pink dawn.

I have taken my chances with weather before.
I was praised by a cartographer once,
he could draw me easily. A meteorologist
set her pen on me and told the world
I was running at eighty knots.
I have almost drowned in rain, spitting hell bubbles
like white kerchiefs. I have burned
almost to nothing in the sun.

Big breasty sun. No one noticed I was growing smaller.
Every day a piece of me removed,
an implacable cauterization. I was accused,
I was the scrap of charcoal she wrote with.
As I shrank, frightened and cold-red, the sun
displayed a terrible visage, she began to laugh.
I was the centre of an atrocity.

What you ask is not simple. Am I happy?
Emotion doesn't measure like a room, yards and inches.
I am happy as a tulip and tell you so.
It's a lie. It's the truth. It's something like plaster
to be molded by the fictioner's tongue.

There are endless worlds in me, acids and sugars.
I am boarded up like a house,
I am free as a star, wheeling the heavens.
Centipedal, I walk on many legs
and one of them, in this storm, tends toward you.

Barbara's Garden
for Sandy

We sat at a restaurant table in 1985
talking of women, of men, of Barbara.
I wanted to move your hand to my lips,
quietly, the smallest of gestures.
It was very beautiful that night: the sky
above Stanley Park freckled with stars,
the candles on our table unwavering.
You spoke of passion, the desire in this world
to make, to stand, to accomplish: how we are counted.
Your mouth was an instrument of great love.

Now I imagine Barbara in her garden:
each spring she lifted the season into light,
turning it to examine corners and mirrors,
its tucked away pulse, listening for the vibration of life.
Barbara at her typewriter, her articulate fight
through the thicket of the body, slashing and burning:
What is wisdom? What is flesh?

You who held this woman in your arms, who laughed
with her, who soothed her sore, troubled passage
know this: her answers were small.
She was the first to speak of time
cut off at the knees, the breasts, tongues.
Later you bent to the necessary tasks,
set your house running, the ragged whir and tick
after Barbara, counting the breaths of your solitude.

You moved through rooms unlocking cabinets and
file drawers, lifting carpets. You opened windows.
You stood in the rain but it was cold.
Your body had ears and eyes, it told the truth.
Waking, not certain it was waking. In Barbara's garden
your hasp of hunger opened, closed, opened.

Berkeley Fire
for Corbin

I know you are reading this poem
I said to Liz I want to understand the trees
I was speaking of eucalyptus in particular
When I met you I said Hello
You said Maybe it will sound ridiculous
but I pray for rain every day here

On the television I saw a woman
shaking hard
I watched her forearms
how she tried to hold herself together
by pressing her elbows on her knees
her face in her hands
Everything else was a still photograph
the still hush of smoke

You are reading this poem
You are rolling a cigarette, or Sharon is
putting flame against your lips
I meant to ask the names of what grows
I said The vegetation is so different
You said I love thunderstorms

Once I passed a burning house
I was safe but I was scared anyway
I didn't understand
how loud, how hot, how big
Later a woman interviewed
standing in the rubble said
It's like being dead then coming back
I'm scared now. I said
You are reading this poem in Berkeley
You said Is it raining?

Thank You
for Candis

1   Cloudy, humid, cool, PMS

I liked Scooby Doo best. My stomach had an appetite I entered for
pleasure. And Fred Astaire. These legs had a different future in
them. Everything that happened happened because I was scared of
my stomach. And legs, what could occur with two.

2   Sunny, hot, humid, waiting for my period

Did I mention besides stomach/legs I was scared of my heart?
Stupid little blood pump sending semaphore, clackety racket, and
no one to decipher. Ginger, backwards.

3   Grey, threat of rain but quiet, period started

I stood on your porch and I was happy about dancing; I was a
maniac of untried steps. Me and Scooby Doo were up. Me and
Scooby with our appetite of dog bones, our tummies floating the
porch supports you'd stained instead of writing stories.

4   Raining, hot, sticky, still bleeding

I was in town because I love you. I was there on my two legs
locked behind words. The body has a vocabulary. Ask Ginger. Ask
Scooby.

5   Still pouring, bleeding but down to one sponge in four hours

Quietly, quietly, you and I body-ing through life, through
letters. Fingers a certain shape for a certain chore. Holding
the pen. The domain of the physical, fingers. The physical
friendship. The ascension on porches, wrapped in your mother's
quilts. The slaked appetite and thank you, on behalf of. My legs
and stomach. Heart.

Adoption
for Melinda

The babies that didn't work
move above their mothers' legs in
somersaults.
Sticky like maple syrup
they stretch the skin
as much as
        labour
they tangle in the arteries
around a heart
wetly beating.

Poor sweetheart
I understand
        how waterlogged –

as if, Melinda, there was choice.

There is
        a scar halving your belly
        a baby lifted out and away

into her life apart   a part of you
swum to life but
leaving you
        breathless.

Leaving you breathless? Melinda, they all do
in our arms or gone   or gone
in the ways they go.

Silver Pennies
for HS

O this ferry dock.
Honesty sighted, Helen,
a plant with stems like
sclerotic arteries
blooming against a green
x-ray screen.
Cough, I coughed.
But here the arbutus shields;
the fish ocean shakes salt over her shoulder.

A good world still,
Helen, a good and gemütlich world.

The dye was a fire
in my brain.
I was burning in effigy,
Helen.
I was burning and coughing
and contemplating the verdict, Helen;
a sandbag on my thigh, blue crosses at each ankle:
my vial of pills in my mouth
like a teat.

The world changes. Nickel and dime,
the big time.

Honesty spits copper pennies.
Helen you kneel
and the little girls hum happinesses:
whistles and toots.
Helen you
talk of the world for mothers, you whisper of
proprioception and war, the Nazi war.
Your paper hands peel
honesties; brown fans of seeds scatter.

O this good world still,
Helen, this good O, good old world.

This ferry dock departure?
What is left on the stalk
is silver and silk, is shells and you
gather it in armfuls.
This is more beautiful than I had hoped, Helen.
I could be wrapped in it, Helen, I
could be buried in
honesty.
Silver pennies on my eyes.

Steam-Cleaning Love
for Cory

This week so much has happened.
Children, the sad flirt of my body
inching to the precipice. I saw you

for the second time. I bought presents
to celebrate the nativity, which I do
from the hollow carved out inside me.

The ordinary things – the red table,
the old chipped countertop, the oranges
on the refrigerator in their Christmas box.

I think of God as a commuter, riding
towards my heart, Her wheels fist-sized,
lighted from within. A steam-cleaning love.

What I meant when I said soul was spirit,
I suppose: or faith, that temptation.
A week like no other (unlike Sundays

in a pew), me standing in the dirty
careless shadow of a cut pine,
you running without weather.

There are gifts: plump stockings
and red paper, the bells of hope,
chocolate and coffee, rain.

I hold birth to your forehead, tonight,
the benediction of the ordinary. The lucky.
I lie beneath you, my arms sliding up

to cradle your slumbrous form, so you
may sleep the dreams of the protected
in the hour of God, in the moment of women.

The Interrogation of Senses
for CD

1 It was simple to dance, the blueprints of love
spread on the floor. There – walls, rooms;
here – the hidden electrical source.
Thinking of lovers, my need is complicated.
I have imagined going to bed as walking
into the breach between fires, the burned-out husks
of trees and houses on each side. Everything rubble
except this hot strip of grass, this sun: you.

2 Call it love. The makeshift variety,
the love that loves raw materials,
that is braver than loneliness.
How I fell through water,
the terrible heat of the two of us pressed.

3 The first act of the new year, the shyly-slipped paper,
the words *I'd like to see you again.*
If I could only look you in the eye, not turn away
even after I am whitewashed by desire,
even after I lower myself towards helplessness,
until we turn together in the adoration of flesh,
in the white bathtub, in the clear, unsoftened light.

4 Later, if we watched the street and argued in pain
and argued men's character, you gripping
your baton, me holding my hands palms up,
even then I would understand I took your life
into my life, an act without complicity.
Even then we would call each other, Refuge.

Entering
for Susan

All day I longed to touch
your hand, which looked rough and sweet.
I passed you the broken nut of a poppy shell.
This was a California poppy, limp and pink,
from a coastal street of blue verandas.
It was a sort of confession, Susan.
I have nothing to distract me. I didn't
think carefully about the loss of the children,
the falling of duties.

I was swallowed by rock at two p.m.
You had already reached Prince George.
I was in Revelstoke, exceeding the speed limit.
I saw a black bear.

The belly of the mountains insists I am small.
Who I am and why here, why you, now?
Will I cry of the child who loses her mother?
The mother walking the shore, hiking the mountains,
the mother in the swimming pool doing laps,
the mother who sits on a single bed writing?

Once, on the first of May, I danced at a Maypole
with my daughter. In the photographs
coloured ribbons fell. Now I am as fearful
of the kiss as you are.
This is a declaration, Susan.
The desire wintered over.
When you called I lifted it like a fuchsia
and pulled peat to see a tender sprouting,
surprising.

In the wallpaper was a hole so small it let you in.
Are you alone? Do you travel
with fathers and priests?
Tell me of when the sun pours down
your cheeks like rain.

This rackety heart, I said.
Raise it up in your field of saplings, Susan.
We love from our marrow
it's the best we can do.
We love from where our fathers have been.
We go under, taking all our breath.

Kiss

for Elise

Oh that kiss in a bottle, messy thing
like egg yolks splatting the floor,
kiss in your kitchen, slippery,
hands and knees sex crawl kiss.

Kiss of nasty girls begging the blender,
the wooden spoon, the wiggly jam.
Filthy slick kiss, cayenne kiss,
kiss of want engorged kiss, buttocks upturned.

Kiss of won't and can't kiss not that kiss.

Orange You
for GW

Be bop beer talk I love you like an orange fountain strip the air
hollow listen to the ache of your notes loads of horn under
dripping trees big bites and tubas, honey, sax and sparking sheets

The beer pours from taps like orange hair, singing that orange
glow after, afterglow I mean, wick of candle hazing orange,
snaptop carrot, what I'm full with

Recreation: First Night

Your eyes
                blue
I didn't want you inside me like that –
I had a cigarette
I held your hands at the wrist
but you drank me, a kind of
Baby Duck
Cheap, I wanted to say
your cheap eyes are
champagne for this poor and
wine for this myopic, but

Give me finger
soft nest of belly
breast
give me fist
I have lots of holes you might plug
even with a tongue, but

Don't make me tremble

bungee jumping

i love to dangle upside down
i love boomerang girls

do jump?
do tease

i i i am three
four five six
picking up the sticks
plumb fall, jolt tall
safety is
a cord, a cord, a cord

i love to bounce
the bounce sugar

shake it down
commercial
belly wobbling elastic

do jump
do flirt
do wet and hot   not
stop?

Jitterbug

Love.
That's what you said
when yours fell over mine
and we were down in a tangle.

We thought it was sweet.
Oh it was!
Your poem girl burst
like camellia blooms.
My dance girl jitterbugged
in a mirror.
Our love girls' lips tumbled
across our skin
like petals or soft rain.

And we went on, somersaulting
our persistent luck.
How we came. We came to nourish
and strengthen,
grafting ourselves by root,
wetting our faces
and thighs
with gladness.

Equinox

We run on and on, on our good feet
Enjambing from sentence to sentence and
room to room, from giggle to snap to pop

I did not know we had so many
preserves put up on creaky
shelves. We open jars rusted tight and
sniff and stare

Much is moldy
overly fruity, overly sour
a kind of vinegar
but still we dip our fingers and suck

In the kitchen my canner boils
the burble of caged glass
The floor is sticky, my feet are
bare and splotted with green

I am sweet
when the trembling recedes
Clockablock clockablock.
What's wrong in my heart
and with schedules
fades

In the garden my back hurt
I was careless
dumping seeds

What ripened?
I didn't know
canning jars had mouths
like the bird babies in the eaves
I didn't know the rap lines
of desperate tomatoes

In my kitchen Etheridge on tape
her tough-stuff songs, my soft-shuffle
and want, I want and want
like a gluttonous –

peach?
carrot?
red thing?

I ate a nasturtium, pink
whose busty seed
my fingers, sweating, once greased and sunk

I harvested five gardens this year, one orchard
and you

Look what a hill I made
for the rock garden. I pose
on it like it was the lake dock –
the dive in my muscles shaping

The summer goes on in me
a drum thrumming
your fingers inside me stroking
all this heat and all this dancing
to ripened vegetables

They aren't safe, I mean
I need winter

The excitation in my blood
concocts a dessert
this knocking, rattling heart spits steam
this do-wop beat across the tile
with my dripping ladle

Fuchsias don't give it up in September
Neither do sweet peas or impatiens
and neither do I
The dahlias and asters wear sun hats –
I wear less and less and
stand before you

I couldn't tell weeds from shoots of cleome
I picked anemones and set them by my bed
It is a question of colour, as always,
when to harvest and what
and what the motivation
and how many teeth will be stained

This rapacious world
sometimes I bite deep

This danger I make from quiet skies
It's tornado season somewhere –
my mother in Florida is evacuated
The storm is not in the air
but don't you notice it rising?

I smell the salt heaving
in from the ocean, I listen
to the weather reports. I want to post a sign –
Small Craft Advisory
Georgia Strait is dangerous

Darling, I want to say I like water
at its roughest
Here is a jar of peaches I skinned
Here am I, ginger root tough and jelly edgy
wanting you
I don't know what I bring
(the storm behind me)   (nothing)
I am indiscriminate, I'll love
anyone who's kind
I am discerning, I love rarely
and rarely enough
Will I forget where you live?

The soil under my nails
is good soil – lead, I think, and toxins
from rain, but good, good as it comes, nurtured

I limber and stretch in front of a mirror
while the late fruit cooks
and the smoke alarm jangles humidity
I have no inhibitions here
with just one reflection

I remember steps that are arcane
I think I remember flirting
and The Jerk and the smell of
my mother's fruit cellar
I think I remember
            how I once was set to go
                  like a top
                        spinning

You are those seedlings
I kissed in May
That spilling bud of July
I am older and just as stupid as –
you? You must be a
knucklehead

I want to come as wet as a woman can
to you
and as hard
I want soft
sauce of apple
I want to be cooked
and sipped like a broth,
put upon you as poultice,
to taste you and see if strawberry
is the word, or raspberry

Do you have a season?
Here the blackberry canes encroach
beyond bounds

The Proposal

Listen to the chocolates
curry favour in the cupboard
calling from their brown cups.
O love, O love, they sing.
The forsythia in the milk pot
squeezes out suns like good mornings,
her hundred yellow lips humming.

The hot smell of sex is in the air.
I have things I must say, mark,
feed into language. About you or myself.
There is an upcoming wedding,
a salmon barbecue in the yard.
Will we? I want to stand beside
you perfectly, repeating

Two women, two women. (I do,
but the kitchen table flicks
her sawhorses like garters.
Now love becomes sleight-of-hand,
a dialect of muscle and skin,
tang and fandango. We speak fluently:
we are starting to mean everything.

Panic Attack

I hold your hand like a
leather shoe, a good walking shoe.
Your hand is an old, old thing,
older than a floor or a wall,

older than yellow.
I slip my finger across creases.
There are fables in your ear.
Behind your knee are poems
blooming in heat haze, lazily.

Tell me of snakes again.
Tell me seven stories.
The woken stir in my gut,
their oceanic waves are yellow.
Your simple hand is as

simple as yellow.
Things that go up are hearts.
I go up in yellow coils
above your fingers.

February 14

Above me you turn like an acrobat
on blue string,
your feet small and accurate.
You are so far away.
My love is not enough to pull you
through the landscaped sky
to this night-wet garden.

It is February.
The bulbs are shooting,
the moon is slipping
dripping stars, hot and sticky.

I am not with you, this simple fact.
Here, I am alone,
climbing from my underground incubation
calling your name
like dewdrop, crocus,
narcissus.
Tonguing the raw tender air.

I miss you. Here and now,
this moment,
my body opens just one way,
the way of the garden moving towards
morning, towards March,
June. Soon spring, that darling –
Soon you, marking every cell of me.

Honey

Honey you twirl around my wrist, a corsage of kisses, a festival of tongues. Honey this is it, this is the one time I want to remember.

Walk it back. I always loved you – say it's true.

When you were born I loved you like a rattle, a teething ring, a mother's breast. When you were three I loved you like a chocolate Easter bunny, eating you ears first, rolling your sugary tips around my mouth. When you were seven I loved you at school, during recess on the jungle gym, hoping for a glimpse up your skirt. At twelve I loved the little nibs of tits rising over your ribs, inviting as suckers.

Walk it forward.

Come on now we've waited so long, take me into you the way girls go, salty and hot. I carry a moon, a bay, an inlet. See how I make pearls from the rough scrapings of boys, the irritations of youth. Honey, it's the middle of the day. I chase us like spilled mercury across a table, taking the temperature of our love, burning up.

Hallowe'en

Ghosts are more real tonight
than you are. Let's say
you are a ghost appearing
above my body in bed
so I can forget about
missing you. I am in this
town and at this curious celebration
changed because of you.

The bonfire is the same.
The fireworks the same
specific pink in a dank
Hallowe'en sky, but I am
somebody else.

Let's say you are milling about
dressed as a pumpkin, round
and orange. Indulge me.
I want to hold you.
The fire is hot up close.
I could singe my eyelashes and
maybe I will, so
someone will notice I'm here.

If Hallowe'en weren't Wednesday
you might be with me. If Hallowe'en
were an easier day for me
I might not mind that
you aren't.

I ought to be able to fly
tonight of all nights
to the simple comfort of your pleasure
in bed, the simple waking, parting
my lips with your simple name.
We wear each other's wombs and dreams
like costumes.

The times I worried about you: when
you were mugged, or in California
on a rugged hillside, or when a lover
struck the bed beside your
trembling body with a stick.

All this fire and noise and
all this put-on character remind
me we arrived like hope.
How many thousands of times already
have I kissed you? You move in me
like laughter. Whatever comes –
more Hallowe'ens, at least – I am
marked by your body and the love
we sailed to accidentally.
Whatever comes after midnight,
the phantoms, the moon, my blackest cat,
this is.

Seaweed

Swimming down into your body I was another woman
altogether, spoiled with rapture. Your shy pink feet were against
my back; you were whispering about rain. I was coming to
Vancouver like a slow wave. You wore your breasts as a necklace:
sliding yourself about my head you said I love you, I love you as I
love apricots. For a moment it was true. I was a beach and you
loved fruit: I turned into a coconut. You broke me open and
drank. Everything was wet. Even the air was watery. You were
very blonde and your eyes were blue. In your ears were seven
circles. I opened your mouth, your thighs, your small shell toes. I
kissed the palm of your hand; fortunes rose like underwater
bubbles and tickled my skin. How I wanted you. I was a dolphin, I
was grey with the surge of your tides and had an
anthropomorphized snout.

You were my first human being.

Sturdies Bay, Galiano Island

I can't look down
the wind is cold
and Jane is on land
and Helen is there
in her garden, tending

I'm sick with the
sea
and my neck
heats
in the sun

there is too much salt
for a happy heart
I don't like spice
I told you
I don't like the
rocking tide
that terrible mother
with whitecaps
all her smells
her adoring eyes

Village Bay, Mayne Island

We are always watching
for the rapist
or the batterer
around the corner
in the mirror
He walks on beautiful legs
He walks pretending tenderness
or laughter
Each lover
is him, walking in
holding the wrist
the breast
insisting herself

To understand charm
is as real as hurt
To understand we wanted love
To understand it happened

I see hurt
the way I see Village Bay
as another stop

Otter Bay, Pender Island

Always
that formal withdrawal
that no to overloaded senses
to confusion and nerves

We were
two idiot savants
spinning plates
rocking
roaming unlined paper
with margins that slid to the right
margins that wobbled
watching

the way autistic kids watch
that slide of eye, that wary glance
The establishment of walls
to stand tall against
to fall against

Watching
the quiver of a city
where darkness stalks

The chattering of tongues
love
the echolalia of desire
and mirrors
and madness

Number games
against comfort
against cold
against the celebratory air

Back, back, I want you back

Panic Attack: Granville Street

City concrete
        like arms to hold me
in, to press against me
like a father

My arched ribs ache
I rock   I tick and tock
This excitation of the blood
this scene
this terrible display

The scream you asked for
hurt so much

I would rather laugh
you understand
I would rather come in my head
imagine fireworks out a window
than let you buy a scream
from the ice cream man
All those pretty bells and pipes

I can't be undone with a rope

Dew-Point

I come home from you by boat,
scenting you on my fingers.
This is a memory; vital,
as our struggle to love is vital,
large with pain.

I touch you knowing how little I know
the wide globe or you. All the books,
all the newscasts bewilder me:
there is an earth and upon it happenings.
In Iraq, war happened
and will not be lost in the arms of
a woman, as I am not lost in yours,
but somehow found and altered.
You happened to me.

You happened to me with life,
that's all, perilously.
You happened to me with
love and the counterpoint
of terror on your streets.
The fire seen from your window;
your thighs opening.
The frightening boys at the rec centre;
your hands on my hair pressing me closer.

A book after all and I learn to read
while I learn to breathe danger
completely
and break like a dew-point over my losses.
Which happened to me. Which are gone.

I stay right here, wherever here is,
learning all over again the unnameable
which I name sorrow and
grief, which I name
gladness and hope.

I stare past the lips of the sea
which the ferry parts –
in the bottom silt a new arithmetic swirls.
My guddled words drip from the railing.
Loving you is a kiss. Of recognition.
Which I have given up,
more scared to try than not try,
in your city, in my country.

I Love You Wildly

The day is fat as an apple.
Fulsome with sun, it's a day for a garden.
My fingers tingle through their earthskins,
though I am still indoors.
My anticipating toes dart like mice,
greedy for soil and air and light,
gluttonous for nematodes.

These are the seedlings I need to bed:
fuchsia, impatiens,
companula, foxglove,
dahlia, phlox,
giving them everything as I have given you –
what?

Sweet green heads,
they are so innocent of autumn.
I love you wildly
from my green heart,
which you say is woody,
like a vine,
rounding your ankles,
twining up.

Give me bone meal.
Give me 18-24-12.
You've pruned me back
like an overzealous laurel,
but I know secrets about fertilizers.

I know roses love garlic.
Together we are stronger;
together we are two parts,
two wholes, and something third,
which is creation.

Air, I Am Air

You write tender poems of violence
in love,
how violence can love a child,
how a lover is a fist
closing over air.

You are that fist,
I am air.

Listen

This is for reckoning.
Look at the ocean's mouth like a mirror,
look at the sumac and her dead flames,
look at the edgy, swaying tulip,
one out of all.

Frantic bells on the porch.
The telephone hides like a child.
Oh my word, oh my mute, mute mouth.
I am more frightened of flowers than anything.

In this homicidal garden,
I hold out the receiver. Listen,
it's a connection for once.
Death by bloom.
It's me, isn't it?
I'm gone,
wagging my lonely stem,
nodding down.

Language Is a Globe in My Throat

The liver has a season, spring.
It has an element, wood.
It has a colour, green.
What lives in the liver is anger.

This is anger's season.
I feel you climbing towards me
as from a storybook,
stepping from the pages of your history,
a valiant anger strapped to your thigh.

If I speak unkindly,
I am not your middle-aged lover
speaking unkindly,
but your past, rearing up.
You have all the anger of years
to unearth, I know,
and you must be diligent.

You approach me already wary,
your hand clapped to the hilt,
your face exactly blank.

Anger is the coin of fear and loss,
which is one currency of love.

Your anger has fallen through a mirror,
into me. I measure its wound
and am horrified. I teeter on the edge of it
trying to sound a word that would locate you,
remember me for you.
I have met anger with anger before;
it is much of what I know how to do,
not enough.
Language is like a globe in my throat,
hot and sore, like the air is hot and sore
with pollutants, like our future: hot and sore
and unspeakable.

Nothing has made this simple, I know.
I look for poultices. Belief in beauty,
compassion.
The strongest is bravery.
My hand extends
over the gully of our estrangement.
Will you reach for it?
If you don't, will I turn away
when turning towards you is what I mean?

Musician

You are my dream lover
nursing my guitar.
I am delicate. Or
I am a wild arpeggio.
All my notes fly up and up.
You stroke me with your tongue,
with your fingers make my chords.
Musician,
I end melodious,
unset to words.

Striped Cat

Here is my room: flamingos,
a Mexican wall,
a small pink pig my daughter made,
cactuses, flowers on the floor.
It is my country, my ship, my one ownable
to dream through.
I ask you to enter, push open the door.

But if the pert fruity lilacs,
the nodding anemones, the pink mallow,
all are fading on the stem,
what will you do?

If you fail to reach me, is anyone to blame?
If we make names – striped cat, yellow pillow –
if we name ourselves
and call what happens happenstance,

if we open the curtains to the sun,
calling faith to the neighbourhood,
calling Love is enough,
will love *be* enough?
What I thought was charted has no map.

Athens at Least

Now the air is clapped shut behind its tin boards.
The rings that sound nowhere toll in my stomach and throat,
like a telephone. You who said Soon are gone,
silent as a bat unhooking from the ceiling.

How intently you swoop and plunge.
Wooing, wooing, you are already over the Atlantic
while I lurch behind, the colour of dishwater,
too soft by half, all muddled, rolling like socks.

Why is the day quiet? Indifferent, exactly like a heart,
pumping and pumping without a word or a cry.
Where is its shriek, its objection, its inflammation?
I sit by like a bone, or a mouth

caught in its act. Bad thing, fleshy mess,
I spill my milk curds, leaking so softly I sicken myself.
I ought to bare my teeth and bring some yellow into it,
I should file a complaint, a writ,

against so much dullness, such dumb stupor.
Bowling pin, I should be struck hard and woken.
After all, it's three, it's late; I am not quite unconscious
no matter what I think. This is a sort of respiration,

a sort of grey breath trying to rattle and jazz.
The disks of my spine are drumming, don't you hear?
Listen. Am I flying? You who are over Athens at least,
should know this is dying, half, and half flying.

Silences

Vertical lover, oscillator, you were the wall
into whose cracks I flowed willingly.
Words can't cure us, you said.
Words are contagious, you said.
You clapped shut your gates, catching my foot
which your henchmother cut clear off.

Vertical lover, instigator, what do you call this?
Clam-like, you slammed tight
and I, treading water, waiting to be your pearl,
said Let's talk and let's talk and let's talk.
My grand salvage operation,
dragging for the corpse of why I bother.

Vertical lover, vascillator, the reason is love,
that unknowable, that ephemeral as air,
that hummingbird I can't lure to the feeder.
Words are air as bullets are air, you said
and bullied up a great storm that shot me
this long way here, too far to reach you.

Vertical lover, constrainer, when I held you
and said Simple as a candle you said
Conflagration, in your throat a rare
red flame. Up in smoke, you said,
laying my language at my feet as tinder,
snapping your match, blazing gone.

Division

I break from a dream of loving you
and think how unintentional we were.
How in this world we joined,
is the surprise. How in this world
we unlinked.
How in this world we willed
such attenuation.

Placing our invertebrate lips
against our pasts
we walked through old loves and fathers like mists.
We walked, our hands uncoupling.
Pain deflated our lungs.
Pain compressed our skulls.
We walked and what was familiar,
understood and explicable,
was that we walked divided.
When you turned to me
I was no lover
but a faceless woman
on whose body
you had wrecked.
When I turned to you
I saw only a stranger.

Every woman is an island,
made so by subterranean heavings.
Every woman floats alone,
the name upon her lips,
loneliness.

How in this world we were scripted
for separation, that women's plot line.
How in this world we tried
to love discerningly.
How in this world we were
sharp-witted and sane
against all odds.
How in this world we found each other.

In My Mind, Cleanly

1 The dog on his house rounds at night
sees we are each in our places,
sees I am in mine,
my bed of years,
where sometimes you have
slept beside me,
and in your sleep reached for me,
and held me, as in the dark
women have always held light.

2 I'm telling the story of my life
as if it were all in the future:
I will be born,
my mother will suckle me,
I will part from her and walk.
In this version,
I plan my growth and womanhood
free of complication.

3 I have touched you,
you have lingered on my skin
and in my mouth
long after memory.
This is my passion,
the lust to contain you
in my body with gentleness,
in my mind cleanly.

4 That photo of the two of us
looking hard into the lens,
your drawings behind us.
Can it be growing colder?
I wake and the unlined paper
is elegy, still unwritten.

5   I am inchoate with longing
to know you in the ways
that in this world
I do not, cannot.
I am stunned
by all I cannot save,
all that's been destroyed
or was discovered, broken.

Paint in Tins

The house is for sale.
The big-bellied sign
sways and sways in the wind.
Pregnant, it carries
a whole family
in its secret womb,
lipping them along like April.
There's even a dog.

One-tracked, stubborn,
I stay put,
feeding my pots verbena.
I won't go anywhere now
til the big show's over,
til the paint is back in its tins,
til the lilacs in the milk pot
grow nostalgic,
flying back to their stumps
to bloom like snow.

In winter it's easy enough –
a house is so small
it's flat as a picture,
covered over with glass.
Like a cat on a shelf
it strokes itself.
It doesn't need me.

But I wake up in March
for the spring juggle.
All the good-hearted trowels
spoon in the shed.
Blameless as a berry,
I pop and sizzle
at the door.

Sweet pea, where are you?
This is our season at last,
whatever the sign says –
For Sale, For Sale,
this is spring.

Love, that old means-everything

1 Last week I sunk a sewing needle
   through my finger.
   Is that what you want, the details?
   Here's a detail for you:
   I slept with someone else.

2 Love.
   That old means-everything, goes-everywhere word.
   I took off your ring.
   Was that love?

3 You're right.
   I have an attitude.

4 My attitude is purple –
   quite florid, it says
   we've been apart
   too long for ease,
   not long enough
   for safety.

Immaculata

Oh mud lover, oh dirt, oh sewage,
I've been wearing April like galoshes,
stomping your ditch
in a swill of brown water,
nursing your weeds like tits.

Well, that's over, it's May tomorrow –
no more quicksand for me.
Is this love, this ooze and stain?
Your leeches ride my elbows.
Your scum exhales me.

Great exhaust, the monoxide
you call admirable
bubbles up from a low extreme,
up from the muck, up from the wallow,
hissing like a let-go fart.

There's a stink, I'm raw from
this virtue, this clean clean clean rape.
Finger of smiles and lies,
I am on to you. Fecal soap,
your brown scrubbing

has a perfectly pious air.
Immaculata of the marsh,
sump pump,
diamond in a quagmire,
how do you rise and rise and rise

in your own estimation?
The trick of caress, say, a masturbation
toxic to others.
Never mind. Up you go, away, away,
dirty incandescence through the sun.

Terra Incognita
for C

All the disappearances
have uneasy names, they drop
like leaves.
It is September's brew,
surprises kept until autumn.

The children wear grief
like too tight ropes.
You didn't stop to explain
flame and rubble
but went as a thief goes
without explanation.

I am equal to the task
of your abandonment.
Your lies pack up their bags
and jabber all night for you.
In the morning I let them out.
They tumble over themselves
to get away, through the yard
screeching your name.
They retain their form
and press their noses to the ground
taking your scent.

I don't know where you are.
I am happy enough for one
morning, with my five dollars
and my needs.

I was trying to see things
in any reasonable way.
I was trying to float.
I thought if the water
was chlorinated. I thought
if summer came. I thought if you
loved me.

Our home is heaving hot breath.
Our home is sweating
like a dancer
without you here.
My body heals in amazing ways.
The bluish tint to my face
is hardly evident at 8 a.m.

You gorge yourself
somewhere
I know
working to satiate.
Working for a reflection
in a mirror.

Someone was meant to die.
That's what I said about
suicide and illness
all our years.
Your threats alarmed me.
Your threats set me up.
Your deceit yanked me up
in a noose.

Weight drops off me. I am
transparent as
an uncooked egg.
Life is not an ugly motive.
It may be noble.
It may wear wellingtons
on two feet.

Lockjaw
for P

hate is not confidential
you arrive with the
rusty taste
of her words
her 42 bad years
on you, transparent
as belief

my septicemia
is five years full
of her raised fist

excuses were everything
lies were the holy beads
she rattled above me
sounding like castanets –
that jazzy
sounding like murmured
prayer, that seductive

pain
is cruelty
with a comely face
good gods
she keeps in her pocket
beside you

you are one of the
pretty maids

she bleeds red dye
from your palms
no one notices
her deceptive rosary
clicking your fingers

Gambling
for C

I was lonely, as alone as a lone woman waiting.
See how I married this house instead of you.
I put it on and wore it like wool socks.
I put it on like a leotard and moped about.
I put it on like a shelf for your books.

This is my wooden wrist writing to you,
scuffed as our weathered oak floor. I wanted
only your attention. I wore a roof on my
head and showed you how my tears leaked down.
I hung wind chimes from my ears.

All the ways and means I had to say I loved you
were lost like dust under sofas.
I found your lips in another town, your
lies in Las Vegas, winning at baccarat.

Aflame
for CJ

I offered you
the love that dares
my rusty tongue flaking stories
and you, your fairy tales
notes on a story, where the next
story is just as true

We began, haltingly
Tales grew essentially

One story we told
was of your husband, a basket
in a clearing, how he
whistled you from the woven shell
of your sisters

The story our foremothers
neglected to inscribe

This love, of woman
and woman, clawing the rockface
with sensate fingers, clawing on
hunger
into blessing
Blazing the summit

Salt Tongues
for CJ

I listened to the sound of your skin
over and over while I was drunk.
It was a gauzy and blue Sunday
on Burrard Inlet; fans of goslings
fell from our ankles like shavings.
The moon lifted the sky, her
hot palm upturned.

I lifted the lick, the bite, the blue
flick salt of love. Was I
right to want the boil and rapture,
the discriminate constellations of your eyes;
you beside me, beyond your
daughters and son,
beyond your husband?

Or to turn you in my arms
as delicately as a bloom turns on its stem
or the ocean turns on its tide? Morning came
and complications gathered in crowds
toting the parasols of our good intentions.
Every time it rained,
I saw trouble.

But I spoke of a kind of marriage
between the fingers of poets,
a conversation of tongues: heads bent,
close on a veil of white,
slipping the zipper, an alphabet
like amulets. Look, exactly here, I said:
the sun spills tender wine.

Sky
for CJ and for Lisa

This is what I meant
and had not the nerve, made small
in my horizon of boxes, how my life
stood undulating and I could not
except one glimpse, could not ...
I was a woman of great extremes
on that bed, that night, I was screaming
folding and opening in origami birds
that bleached in sunlight
electrifying paper wings.

I would not have brought him
stringing him by his ashy, sticky hand to our love
if there'd been choice or control. You were warm,
the slots of your ribs like a boat to ride.
Who has not listened when one should not?
The archaeology of my father, can I tell you
he is dead by his own hand, and twenty years?
This is the incantation of the poem, which sings
into fear, on the shore, in the bed, the mess
of the potsherd and shovel, the tools in the sand digging:
always him. And I hate
for the cost of him to my life.

I twisted for sweetness, touched you, lip to lip
the tug of the crustacean loosing her shell
the excavation of your brown eyes.
The children's birthday party
seemed an innocent memory: the little
shorn girl I was, my winking father
the ponies pulling kids for nickel rides.
A child of July, like you, a horoscope
of heat and mosquitoes. I tongued
your nipples but found no harbour
set no anchor in the fishy moistness of thigh
the parting of your breath.
Always the crisp birds rising
the hard blue feral spark, the sky:
in the end scared cold.

Trash
for G

The story of me is in garbage bins –
lazy flies spin the neighbourhood.
I am not proud but I am not ashamed,
which is what you require for penance.

It was an idyll, this all-sorts family
for a year. Now it's over. Your mouth
has eaten me. The dead rock their ears.

I am loose pages, coffee-stained.
I am sorted against recycling.
I am still the very same woman
you loved irretrievably.

Rising
for Edna

It is October, that hell month
where my friend Diane
softens my lips to kiss her children,
kneads my hands to bake her bread,
moves my legs to get her walking done.
It's only four weeks, October,
plus a little bit. Four weeks
of changing clocks, of sparklers
moaning on the streets. Let Diane
tell you, using my tongue, gibbling
her story with my larynx and these
ugly teeth. I am tired of bravery.
I refuse to be blessed, piggybacking
my dead friend. I refuse to learn a thing
about forgiveness: the body of a young mother
is gone, that's all.

Mother of three.
I put on my hat. I draw on my shoes.
I stand in the shower fully clothed.
Look in the garden, Edna –
a window box of bruises howls
good morning.

Horseshoes
for JdL

The night slipped its blinders.
I rode bareback to another room.
It had been nine years since I kissed
the emeralds from your eyes.
I climbed your body again,
willingly, clasping a favourite horseshoe.

All around, I remember, were clouds
like saddles and promises. I missed
primary colours and numbers, I missed myself.
Luck was turning her cheek.

Your body, dipping, pulled my cry
into the uncut light – ugly
despite my talismans,
the dull sad brown of a mare's eye.
I hated it. I was there
only to prove something. The orange
hotel room blankets were up to my neck.
The way bodies can be betrayals,
no name of God whispering under our hair,
wrapping our wrists, sliding out from our thighs.

I put my tears under my cheek,
planted them like seeds there,
where they stayed unseen. You never saw them.
You were a woman and I, woman.
My body was hot, sore and trembling,
the city outside the windows smelled of rape.

It was autumn. I released myself
woman by woman. In my mind
a herd was galloping through a fire.
I unlinked the bridles, the bits, the cinches.
I smashed the horseshoes.
I tore the lust from my body
and bled from my lips. The thick smell of sex
was the noise of hooves and smoke.
All my mistakes were born like fillies
suckling up to teats of ash.

Ladder
for GF

It was the ladder I saw,
the raw clop of hammer and nail,
the wordless, tedious years between
the provinces, between the scars
and who you think I am.
My hunger was unavoidable, though
you assailed it. My laughter was dense,
a terrified thing running.
It was the placement of rungs too far between
or the six years of mornings
or the miles of provinces.

Your hips, drawing them over and over,
tongue to skin like pencil.
I didn't know what I wanted.
Love. A plane ticket away.

The Pause Between Us
for BF

1 I am sorry for your dog,
crying towards upstairs. I am sorry
for water on the bathroom floor.
I am sorry for the electricity which
ate at the basement hole. I
am sorry for the woman who wore black and purple
and I am sorry I could not lift the
soot stain from the ceiling.

The moment before sleep, the past is
a lovely whiteness, a rip in the bed.

2 A long girl, with vaporous weight, with
sad, stretched limbs. You weren't bad,
just lonely. You'd climb into my car
if I was travelling west. Or east.
If I was perfect I could drive you
through the wasteland of your spirit
til my gas ran out.

3 I am sorry for the tending of debts
while the sun burned brilliant
as water to drown in,
brilliant as glass to scratch,
urgent and powerful. I am sorry
I stopped listening when the TV
tuned to static. I
am sorry for the dedication.

I am sorry for my friends. I am
sorry for the cherry stone
I swallowed, rooting hard and long, gushing a
wheeze of milk, filling the pause between us.

4 You sat in your truck, my brake lights smashed
   and you were not sorry. You walked from
   the woods and woke me and you
   were not sorry. You etched my name
   on your palms and were not sorry. You
   drew me as if I were your child, a
   concoction of you, a devilment, and were not sorry.

   My unadorned faith. This chore
   of loving you is my faith. This purpose is you,
   unadorned.

Across Horizons
for C

Love, you who carry me through infirmity,
I cannot answer you more than weakly, my words
lifting from my mouth in shades of rose and violet,
full of sulphurous hope, to be allowed, to live.

Oh my small small voice. My churlish heart
never melted, the feverish beat captured in cement,
the thick, greasy pump suspicious and fretful
below it. The tree of me is dying: I need you.

In the end, between us, the greedy suck of my love –
I am trying to speak of gratitude, to breathe
the webbed mystery of my life and death, eagerly, to say
I have been lost, and found again, by you dear.

But this frail expulsion hurls me to regrets
that fall like our daughters' dominos, or like suns
we have watched dive into night graves, their beaks
pecking the end of days, spreading blood across horizons.

Appropriation
for Bonnie

I open my mouth over privilege.
The air stains blue and bruises
the mockery of your blood-pump,
how you have said, Please, please
don't.

I shrink you til you unhook your brain,
remove your bones, snap loose your toes;
but am I happy? I drink sherry:
it eases the fit.

I open my white, clean fingers
and gather stones from your kidneys.
You were almost invisible til I wore you
here, to cocktails, at the podium,
in the thong around my neck.

You say, Please.

Jericho
for Jane

Today my daughter and I at Jericho Beach.
It's October; we look for words to describe
the smell of fallen leaves we walk through.
This is a memory already, for Meghann.
My mother and I used to feed coots, she'll say
and used to tease flying seagulls, tossing
bread to the sky for them to catch mid-air.

To say I am born, Jane, studying my life
in my daughter's face, in the barge, in the blue,
in the father and his girls playing soccer
is true: practising til strength, or sense
or what I've come to call perspective.

They're mostly good people, you said
of my literary contacts, and I've forgotten
humanity too often, preferring the argument,
the jargon, the shell of my ocean life
to close over me. I forget that to cry helplessly
is a wasted motion. Open the letters. Dock at your
words, each page a wave salted with love.

Paper and Ink
for A

It was simple at the beginning.
Begin at the beginning.
You took my hand and began me
in your bed
with your body.

I laughed then, full-throatedly.
I mean this exactly.
You knew exactly
the map I'd left in the night
visible to your blue eyes.

Your name started at my lips
and trickled down my body til
you were inside me
and how could that be?
I wrote the next story
on your skin, a spiral of stories
inscribed by my tongue.
You were paper, I was ink.

Curled with a pearl
against your stomach,
that giddiness of fatigue
and rocking horses and strong backs,
you unfolded a silver pirouette.

You put an apple on my cheek.
It wasn't the season for ripeness
of course
but what patience I had.

Remembering your lips:
arched over you in bed
the way I rose.
All my cells were up and dancing,
wearing white tuxedos.

Perhaps this is the moment, then,
to speak of love again,
dressing her differently.

Concerning your letter:
each pore cried the change of light.
I held the trembling bells of you
to my fingertips.

Elemental
for Kathy

I'll dance with the heron
on the ice floe
wearing my best blue gown.
I'll catch a wave in my mouth.
I'll eat yellow. I'll turn on the sun
til she pours liquid heat. All
the oxygen in the world
will hopscotch to my legs.
I'll cha-cha giggling and sugar kiss
the toes of babies. I'll plant flowers.
I'll ignite the winter sky
with spoonfuls of hope.
I'll sound like a flute
and the stars will be candles
and the air will be a green symphony.
I'll call happiness from trees,
from ponds, from bonfires,
from mountains;
I'll call love.

Notes

The dedication line is borrowed from and used by permission of Kathy Shaidle, a Toronto writer.

'the body's memory'
The poem was provoked by Diana Kemble's painting of the same name, half of which illustrated the cover of *Body Rain*. The painting was lost in a warehouse fire.

'Barbara's Garden'
For Sandra Butler, author of *Cancer in Two Voices,* a response to our friendship and the loss of her lover to breast cancer.

'Silver Pennies'
For Helen Sonthoff, who lives on Galiano Island and whose presence, while quiet, reminds me of how lucky life is.

'Rising'
For Edna Alford, with whom I've had several provocative discussions. About Diane Corkum, murdered Oct. 29/89.

'Jericho'
For Jane Rule who cautions me to be more humane.

'Elemental'
For Kathy Shaidle, a woman who holds my hand.

J.A. Hamilton is the author of *Jessica's Elevator*, a children's book, *Body Rain*, a collection of poetry and *July Nights and Other Stories*, a collection of short fiction. Her work has appeared in such places as the *New York Times* and *Seventeen* magazine. In 1992, she was runner-up for the Pat Lowther Award, the VanCity Book Award and the Ethel Wilson Fiction Prize in the B.C. Book Awards. She won the 1992 Federation of B.C. Writers Literary Writes Competition and an award in the 1992 Prism International short fiction contest.